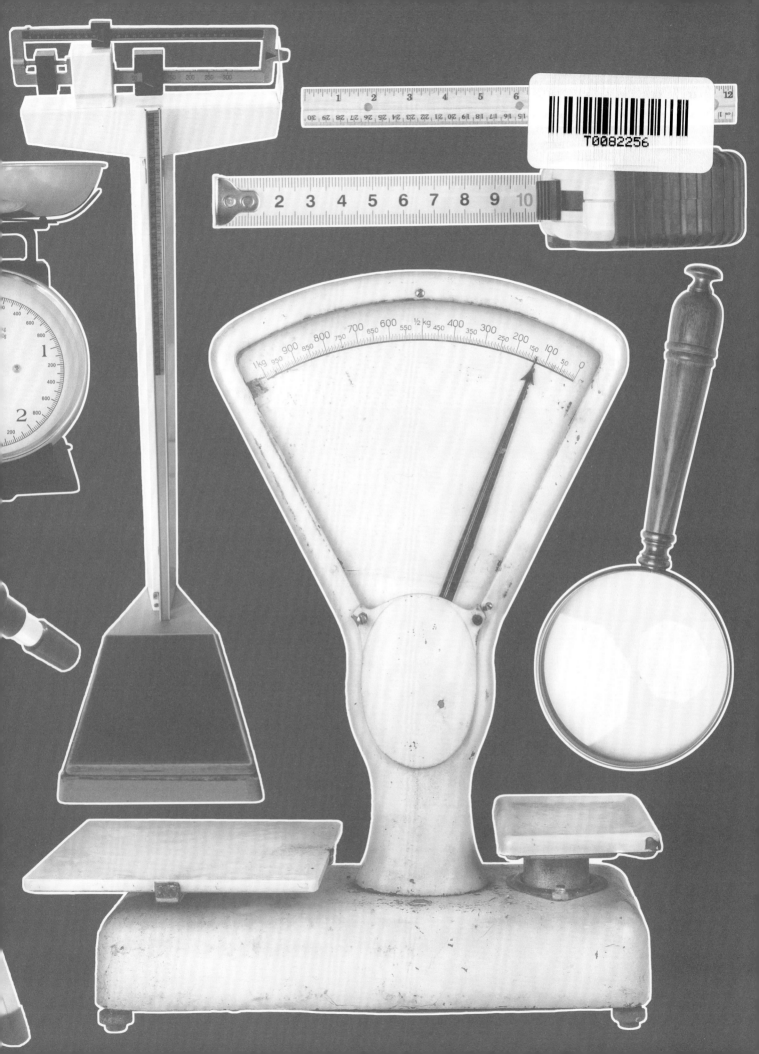

THE SIZE OF EVERYTHING

GINORMOUS GALAXIES, ITTY-BITTY QUARKS, AND ME

written by
ALYSSA CLEMENTS

illustrated by
ANGELIKA SCUDAMORE

TYNDALE KIDS

Tyndale House Publishers
Carol Stream, Illinois

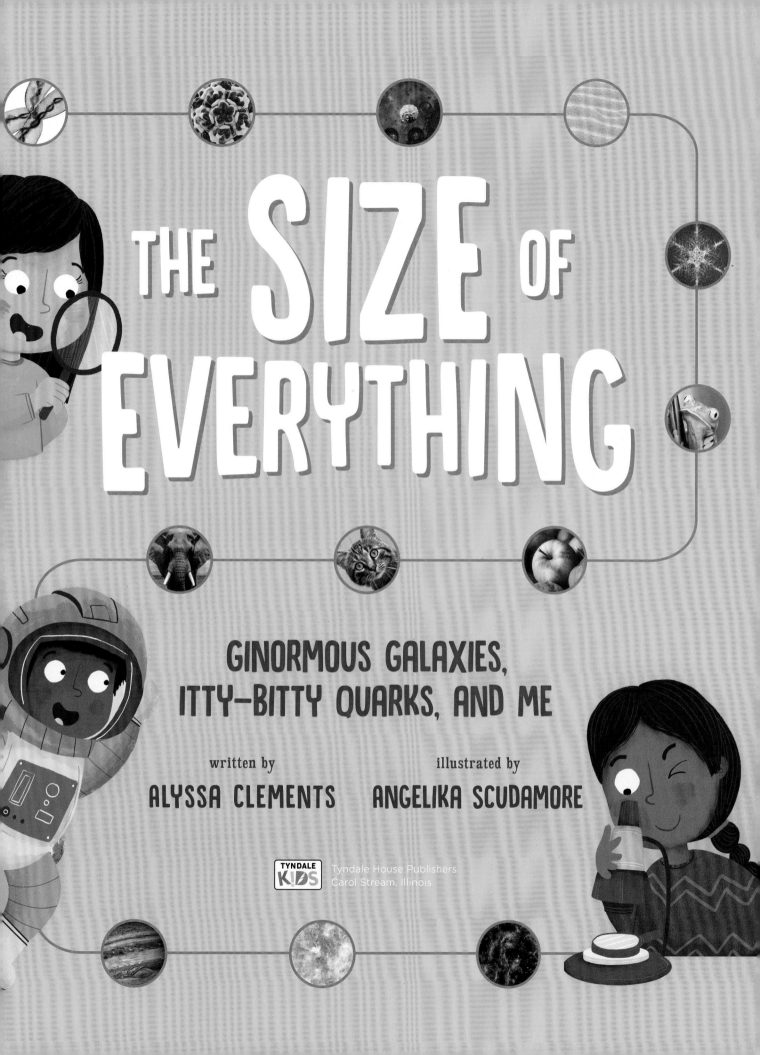

FOR
MY CHILDREN,
MAY YOU ALWAYS KNOW
HOW INFINITELY GOD
LOVES YOU!

Visit Tyndale's website for kids at tyndale.com/kids.

Tyndale is a registered trademark of Tyndale House Ministries.
The Tyndale Kids logo is a trademark of Tyndale House Ministries.

The Size of Everything: Ginormous Galaxies, Itty-Bitty Quarks, and Me

Designed by Julie Chen

For manufacturing information regarding this product, please call 1-855-277-9400.

For information about special discounts for bulk purchases, please contact Tyndale House Publishers at csresponse@tyndale.com, or call 1-855-277-9400.

Library of Congress Cataloging-in-Publication Data

A catalog record for this book is available from the Library of Congress.

ISBN 978-1-4964-6253-4

Printed in China

29	28	27	26	25	24	23
7	6	5	4	3	2	1

Special thanks to Arend J. Poelarends, PhD, and Coreen Ogilvie, MAT, for sharing your knowledge and love of science with this book.

READ THIS FIRST

This book is not like other books. It begins in the middle! In order for you to understand just how big and small different parts of God's creation are, it's helpful to start with the size of something that you know really well—yourself! Look down at your body and think about how big you are. Then flip ahead to the middle of this book to begin to see how your size compares to the incredible world God has made.

QUARK

THE QUARK IS THE SMALLEST OBJECT IN THE UNIVERSE THAT WE KNOW ABOUT. EACH PROTON OR NEUTRON IS MADE OF THREE QUARKS.

We know the quark exists based on experiments, but it is so small that it's never actually been measured. Isn't it amazing that God came up with the idea to create something so tiny? And he sees and understands exactly how it works!

There are six different kinds of quarks. Scientists call them flavors, but these flavors are too small to taste!

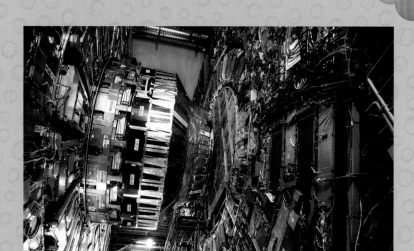

A particle accelerator uses magnets to smash parts of atoms together at super high speeds, which causes quarks to pop out. The only place scientists can see quarks is in here.

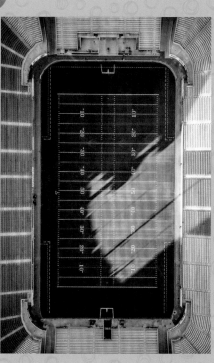

The largest particle accelerator in the world is longer than 295 American football fields!

SMALLER

Quark
Electron
Proton and Neutron
Atom
DNA Unit
Common Cold Virus
X Chromosome
White Blood Cell
Thickness of a Human Hair
Grain of Sand
Largest Bacteria
Snow Crystal
Ant
Poison Dart Frog
Chicken Egg
Apple
Hercules Beetle
Ear of Corn
Queen Alexandra's Birdwing
Chihuahua
Cat
Beaver
Rafflesia
Emperor Penguin
Chinese Giant Salamander

Why would God create something that we can't even see or measure? The Bible says that all of creation exists to show how incredible God is and to point us to him.

If you ever feel small or unimportant, just remember that God created itty-bitty, super-small quarks, and they make him happy. If he sees and rejoices in things so small, he definitely sees and loves YOU—the one he created special in his own image to be his friend and enjoy his fascinating world!

ELECTRON

A PARTICLE FILLED WITH ELECTRICITY THAT SPEEDS AROUND THE PROTONS AND NEUTRONS INSIDE OF AN ATOM

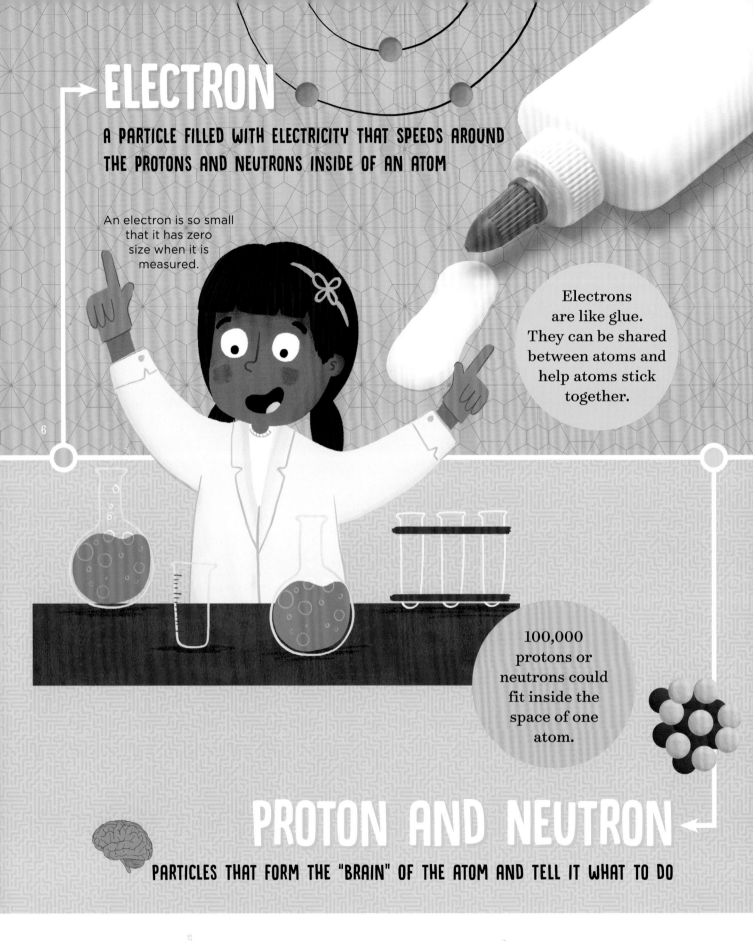

An electron is so small that it has zero size when it is measured.

Electrons are like glue. They can be shared between atoms and help atoms stick together.

100,000 protons or neutrons could fit inside the space of one atom.

PROTON AND NEUTRON

PARTICLES THAT FORM THE "BRAIN" OF THE ATOM AND TELL IT WHAT TO DO

SMALLER

Quark | Electron | Proton and Neutron | Atom | DNA Unit | Common Cold Virus | X Chromosome | White Blood Cell | Thickness of a Human Hair | Grain of Sand | Largest Bacteria | Snow Crystal | Ant | Poison Dart Frog | Chicken Egg | Apple | Hercules Beetle | Ear of Corn | Queen Alexandra's Birdwing | Chihuahua | Cat | Beaver | Rafflesia | Emperor Penguin | Chinese Giant Salamander

ATOM

A SMALL BUILDING BLOCK
THAT MAKES UP EVERYTHING IN THE UNIVERSE

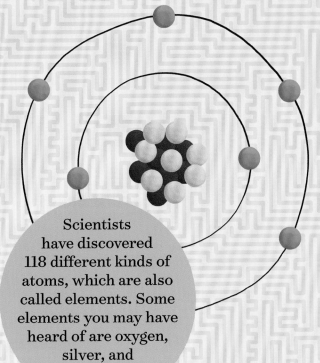

An adult's body is made of around 7 octillion atoms. That's a 7 followed by 27 zeros (7,000,000,000,000,000,000,000,000,000)!

Scientists have discovered 118 different kinds of atoms, which are also called elements. Some elements you may have heard of are oxygen, silver, and gold.

Each person's DNA is one of a kind. There will never be another person exactly like you!

Your DNA comes from your parents and determines what you look like. This includes your eye color, hair color, height, and even if you have freckles or not.

There are so many of these tiny DNA pieces in your body that if you lined them up next to each other, they could stretch from the Earth to the edge of the solar system 7 times!

DNA UNIT

A RECIPE THAT EXPLAINS HOW A LIVING THING WILL WORK

8-Year-Old Child · Giant Earthworm · Wandering Albatross · Elephant · Tyrannosaurus Rex · Blue Whale · Redwood Tree · Angel Falls · Uluru · Humongous Fungus · Mount Everest · Mariana Trench · Grand Canyon · Olympus Mons · Moon · Earth · Jupiter · Sun · VY Canis Majoris · The Solar System · Crab Nebula · Tarantula Nebula · Milky Way Galaxy · BOSS Great Wall · **BIGGER**

COMMON COLD VIRUS

A GERM THAT GIVES YOU A SORE THROAT AND A RUNNY NOSE

It is often called the *rhinovirus*, but it's much smaller than a rhino!

8

About 70 X chromosomes could fit on one grain of sand.

Girls have two X chromosomes.

Boys have an X and a Y chromosome.

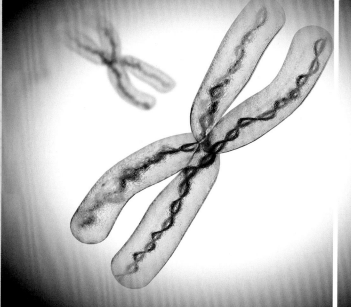

X CHROMOSOME

A SET OF INSTRUCTIONS FOR YOUR BODY

SMALLER

Quark · Electron · Proton and Neutron · Atom · DNA Unit · **Common Cold Virus** · **X Chromosome** · **White Blood Cell** · **Thickness of a Human Hair** · Grain of Sand · Largest Bacteria · Snow Crystal · Ant · Poison Dart Frog · Chicken Egg · Apple · Hercules Beetle · Ear of Corn · Queen Alexandra's Birdwing · Chihuahua · Cat · Beaver · Rafflesia · Emperor Penguin · Chinese Giant Salamander

WHITE BLOOD CELL

A CELL THAT FLOATS IN YOUR BLOOD AND FIGHTS GERMS

Over 100 white blood cells could fit in the period at the end of this sentence.

Many white blood cells only live for one to three days, but don't worry! Your body is always making more of them.

Melanin is what gives your hair its color. The more melanin your hair has, the darker it will be.

About 50 to 100 hairs fall off your head every day.

The distance from *here* to *here*

THICKNESS OF A HUMAN HAIR

8-Year-Old Child
Giant Earthworm
Wandering Albatross
Elephant
Tyrannosaurus Rex
Blue Whale
Redwood Tree
Angel Falls
Uluru
Humongous Fungus
Mount Everest
Mariana Trench
Grand Canyon
Olympus Mons
Moon
Earth
Jupiter
Sun
VY Canis Majoris
The Solar System
Crab Nebula
Tarantula Nebula
Milky Way Galaxy
BOSS Great Wall

BIGGER

GRAIN OF SAND

A MINI PIECE OF ROCK THAT CAN BE FOUND AT THE BEACH

Sand dunes form when wind blows grains of sand into large hills.

A person who collects different kinds of sand is called an arenophile.

Its scientific name is *Thiomargarita namibiensis* (thi-oh-mar-gah-REE-tah nah-mih-be-EN-sis).

Most bacteria aren't dangerous, but some can make you sick. This is why it's important to wash your hands.

This bacteria is about the same size as one poppyseed in a poppyseed muffin.

LARGEST BACTERIA

A GERM THAT LIVES IN THE OCEAN AND CAN BE SEEN WITHOUT A MICROSCOPE

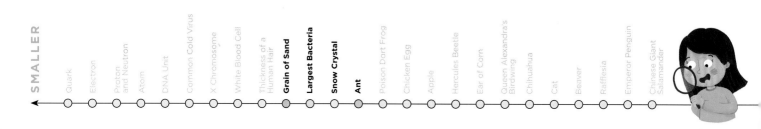

SMALLER

Quark · Electron · Proton and Neutron · Atom · DNA Unit · Common Cold Virus · X Chromosome · White Blood Cell · Thickness of a Human Hair · **Grain of Sand** · **Largest Bacteria** · **Snow Crystal** · **Ant** · Poison Dart Frog · Chicken Egg · Apple · Hercules Beetle · Ear of Corn · Queen Alexandra's Birdwing · Chihuahua · Cat · Beaver · Rafflesia · Emperor Penguin · Chinese Giant Salamander

SNOW CRYSTAL

ICE THAT FALLS FROM A CLOUD

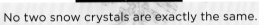

Every snow crystal has six points that grow out from its middle.

No two snow crystals are exactly the same.

The largest ant colony in the world is home to about 307 million ants and stretches over 6,000 kilometers. That's larger than the distance across the Atlantic Ocean!

Ants have two stomachs: one stomach for eating and one stomach for holding food to share with other ants.

ANT

AN INSECT THAT LIVES IN LARGE GROUPS CALLED COLONIES

POISON DART FROG

A BRIGHTLY COLORED FROG WHOSE SKIN IS POISONOUS

Its bright colors warn other animals not to eat it.

These frogs are about the same size as a US quarter.

It takes 21 days for a baby chick to hatch.

CHICKEN EGG

AN EGG LAID BY A HEN

Hens can lay one egg each day.

SMALLER

Quark | Electron | Proton and Neutron | Atom | DNA Unit | Common Cold Virus | X Chromosome | White Blood Cell | Thickness of a Human Hair | Grain of Sand | Largest Bacteria | Snow Crystal | Ant | **Poison Dart Frog** | **Chicken Egg** | **Apple** | **Hercules Beetle** | Ear of Corn | Queen Alexandra's Birdwing | Chihuahua | Cat | Beaver | Rafflesia | Emperor Penguin | Chinese Giant Salamander

APPLE

A FRUIT THAT GROWS IN AN ORCHARD

There are over 7,500 varieties of apples.

Most apples have around 10 seeds.

The Hercules beetle can carry up to 850 times its own weight. That's like carrying 850 of your friends all at the same time!

A Hercules beetle is about the same size as a dinner fork.

HERCULES BEETLE

THE STRONGEST INSECT

8-Year-Old Child · Giant Earthworm · Wandering Albatross · Elephant · Tyrannosaurus Rex · Blue Whale · Redwood Tree · Angel Falls · Uluru · Humongous Fungus · Mount Everest · Mariana Trench · Grand Canyon · Olympus Mons · Moon · Earth · Jupiter · Sun · VY Canis Majoris · The Solar System · Crab Nebula · Tarantula Nebula · Milky Way Galaxy · BOSS Great Wall

BIGGER

EAR OF CORN
A GRAIN THAT GROWS ON A TALL STALK

Each ear of corn has about 800 kernels.

An ear of corn is about the same length as a business envelope.

Although most corn is yellow, some farmers also grow black, blue, purple, green, red, and white corn.

These butterflies live on only one island in Papua New Guinea.

Their wingspan is larger than a basketball.

QUEEN ALEXANDRA'S BIRDWING
THE LARGEST BUTTERFLY

SMALLER

Quark · Electron · Proton and Neutron · Atom · DNA Unit · Common Cold Virus · X Chromosome · White Blood Cell · Thickness of a Human Hair · Grain of Sand · Largest Bacteria · Snow Crystal · Ant · Poison Dart Frog · Chicken Egg · Apple · Hercules Beetle · **Ear of Corn** · **Queen Alexandra's Birdwing** · **Chihuahua** · **Cat** · Beaver · Rafflesia · Emperor Penguin · Chinese Giant Salamander

CHIHUAHUA

THE WORLD'S SMALLEST DOG

Chihuahuas are named after the state of Chihuahua, Mexico.

A Chihuahua is about 8 centimeters shorter than a bowling pin.

Cats love to snooze! Most sleep for 12 to 16 hours per day.

A group of cats is called a clowder.

CAT

A COMMON PET

8-Year-Old Child · Giant Earthworm · Wandering Albatross · Elephant · Tyrannosaurus Rex · Blue Whale · Redwood Tree · Angel Falls · Uluru · Humongous Fungus · Mount Everest · Mariana Trench · Grand Canyon · Olympus Mons · Moon · Earth · Jupiter · Sun · VY Canis Majoris · The Solar System · Crab Nebula · Tarantula Nebula · Milky Way Galaxy · BOSS Great Wall

BIGGER

BEAVER

A RODENT THAT CHEWS DOWN TREES IN ORDER TO BUILD LARGE HOMES CALLED DAMS

Beavers have flat, paddle-shaped tails that can be as long as a rolling pin and are used for swimming and slapping the water to scare away predators.

The largest beaver dam in the world is so large that it can be seen from space! The amount of water it holds would fill 92,000 dump trucks.

They smell like rotten meat in order to attract helpful insects. Yuck!

The diameter of the rafflesia is about the same size as a standard toy Hula-Hoop!

RAFFLESIA

THE LARGEST FLOWER

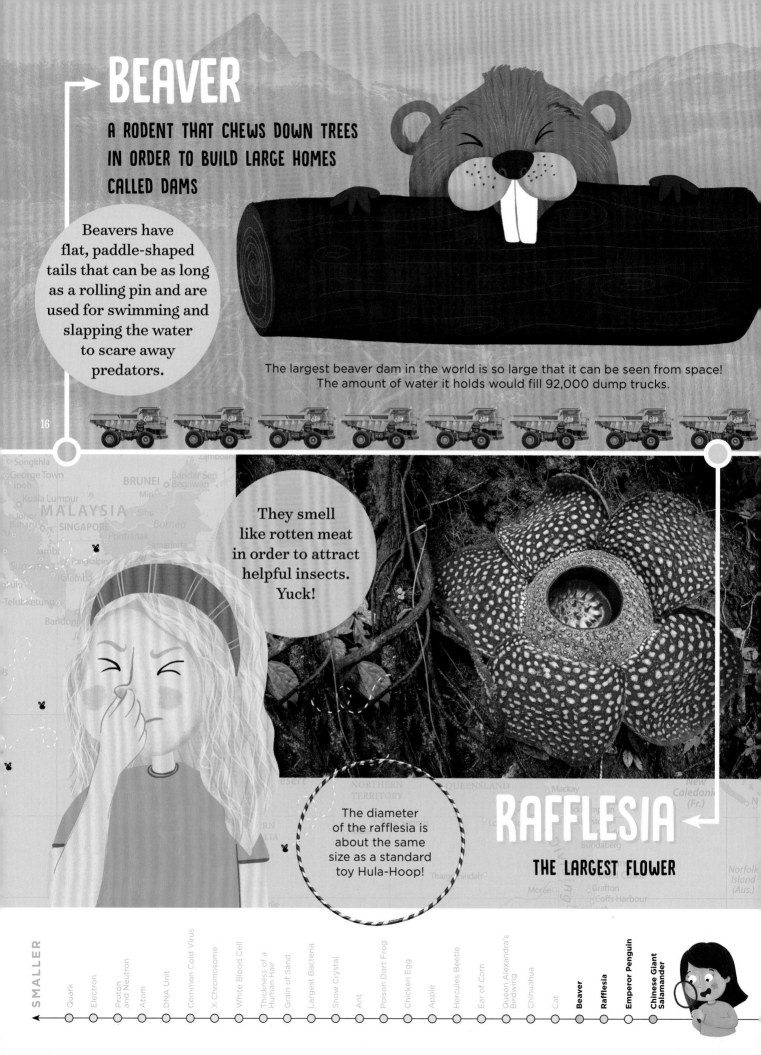

SMALLER

Quark · Electron · Proton and Neutron · Atom · DNA Unit · Common Cold Virus · X Chromosome · White Blood Cell · Thickness of a Human Hair · Grain of Sand · Largest Bacteria · Snow Crystal · Ant · Poison Dart Frog · Chicken Egg · Apple · Hercules Beetle · Ear of Corn · Queen Alexandra's Birdwing · Chihuahua · Cat · **Beaver** · **Rafflesia** · **Emperor Penguin** · **Chinese Giant Salamander**

EMPEROR PENGUIN

THE TALLEST AND HEAVIEST PENGUIN

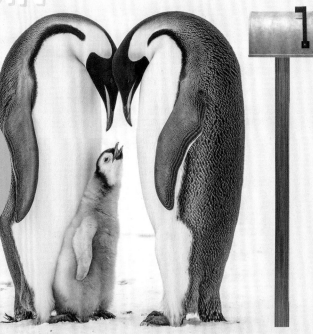

Dad penguins hold their eggs on their feet for two months without eating anything until their babies hatch.

Adult emperor penguins are the height of a standard mailbox.

They live underwater and breathe through their skin.

These salamanders are about the same size as two standard bed pillows laying next to each other.

These salamanders are critically endangered, which means there are only a few of them still alive.

CHINESE GIANT SALAMANDER

THE LARGEST AMPHIBIAN IN THE WORLD

8-Year-Old Child · Giant Earthworm · Wandering Albatross · Elephant · Tyrannosaurus Rex · Blue Whale · Redwood Tree · Angel Falls · Uluru · Humongous Fungus · Mount Everest · Mariana Trench · Grand Canyon · Olympus Mons · Moon · Earth · Jupiter · Sun · VY Canis Majoris · The Solar System · Crab Nebula · Tarantula Nebula · Milky Way Galaxy · BOSS Great Wall

BIGGER

DID YOU KNOW THAT GOD CREATED EVERYTHING IN THE ENTIRE UNIVERSE?

A long, long, long time ago, nothing existed except for God. But then God turned the nothing into billions of amazing things. Everything in the whole universe has been created by him. The weird bugs and the beautiful mountains. The tiny cells and the ginormous galaxies. They all exist because God specifically chose to make them, and afterward, he said that they were all good.

But did you know that out of everything God created, he made one thing more special than all the rest—one thing that he called very good? He made **YOU!** And he made you different from anything else he had made—he made you to be like him! The Bible calls this *being created in God's image*.

God made people to be his friends and told them to learn about the incredible world he created and to take care of it. You can read about this in the Bible in Genesis 1 and 2. As you flip through this book, you will see just how big and amazing God's creation is, and how big and amazing God is for creating it all!

TURN THIS PAGE TO WATCH GOD'S CREATION GET SMALLER AND SMALLER!

SMALLER

Quark · Electron · Proton and Neutron · Atom · DNA Unit · Common Cold Virus · X Chromosome · White Blood Cell · Thickness of a Human Hair · Grain of Sand · Largest Bacteria · Snow Crystal · Ant · Poison Dart Frog · Chicken Egg · Apple · Hercules Beetle · Ear of Corn · Queen Alexandra's Birdwing · Chihuahua · Cat · Beaver · Rafflesia · Emperor Penguin · Chinese Giant Salamander

START READING HERE

TURN THIS PAGE TO WATCH GOD'S CREATION GET BIGGER AND BIGGER!

8-Year-Old Child

Giant Earthworm

Wandering Albatross

Elephant

Tyrannosaurus Rex

Blue Whale

Redwood Tree

Angel Falls

Uluru

Humongous Fungus

Mount Everest

Mariana Trench

Grand Canyon

Olympus Mons

Moon

Earth

Jupiter

Sun

VY Canis Majoris

The Solar System

Crab Nebula

Tarantula Nebula

Milky Way Galaxy

BOSS Great Wall

BIGGER

GIANT EARTHWORM

A WORM THAT LIVES UNDERGROUND IN AUSTRALIA

INDIAN OCEAN

These worms can grow up to nine and a half feet (three meters) long!

That's the same size as three guitars laid next to each other.

They can travel for over a year without touching land.

An albatross's wingspan is wider than the length of a hopscotch court (by about one foot).

WANDERING ALBATROSS

THE BIRD WITH THE LARGEST WINGSPAN

SMALLER

Quark • Electron • Proton and Neutron • Atom • DNA Unit • Common Cold Virus • X Chromosome • White Blood Cell • Thickness of a Human Hair • Grain of Sand • Largest Bacteria • Snow Crystal • Ant • Poison Dart Frog • Chicken Egg • Apple • Hercules Beetle • Ear of Corn • Queen Alexandra's Birdwing • Chihuahua • Cat • Beaver • Rafflesia • Emperor Penguin • Chinese Giant Salamander

ELEPHANT

THE LARGEST LIVING LAND ANIMAL

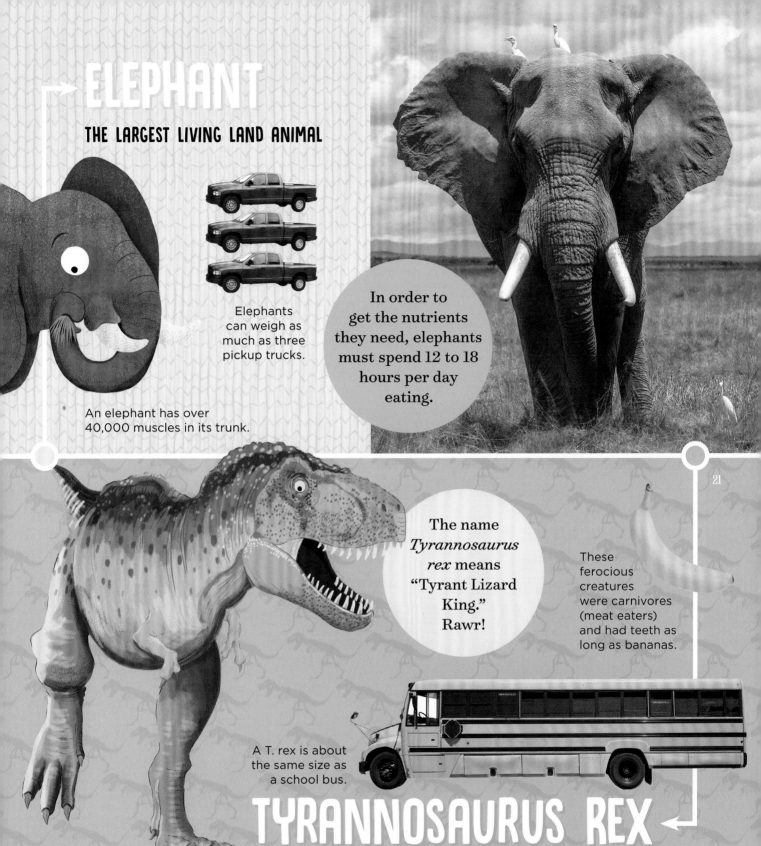

Elephants can weigh as much as three pickup trucks.

An elephant has over 40,000 muscles in its trunk.

In order to get the nutrients they need, elephants must spend 12 to 18 hours per day eating.

The name *Tyrannosaurus rex* means "Tyrant Lizard King." Rawr!

These ferocious creatures were carnivores (meat eaters) and had teeth as long as bananas.

A T. rex is about the same size as a school bus.

TYRANNOSAURUS REX

A DINOSAUR WITH A LARGE HEAD AND TAIL AND UNUSUALLY SHORT FRONT LEGS

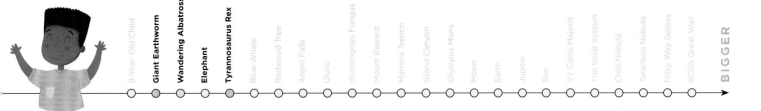

8-Year-Old Child · **Giant Earthworm** · **Wandering Albatross** · **Elephant** · **Tyrannosaurus Rex** · Blue Whale · Redwood Tree · Angel Falls · Uluru · Humongous Fungus · Mount Everest · Mariana Trench · Grand Canyon · Olympus Mons · Moon · Earth · Jupiter · Sun · VY Canis Majoris · The Solar System · Crab Nebula · Tarantula Nebula · Milky Way Galaxy · BOSS Great Wall

BIGGER

BLUE WHALE

THE LARGEST ANIMAL

A blue whale's heart is as big as a car.

An adult blue whale can grow to be longer than a basketball court.

H. H. Barnes Team In Redwood Tree

A redwood tree can live for more than 2,000 years.

A redwood tree can grow as tall as 19 giraffes standing on top of each other!

Groups of redwood trees twist their roots together underground. This helps the trees to not fall over.

REDWOOD TREE

A VERY TALL TREE WITH RED BARK AND SMALL CONES

SMALLER

Quark · Electron · Proton and Neutron · Atom · DNA Unit · Common Cold Virus · X Chromosome · White Blood Cell · Thickness of a Human Hair · Grain of Sand · Largest Bacteria · Snow Crystal · Ant · Poison Dart Frog · Chicken Egg · Apple · Hercules Beetle · Ear of Corn · Queen Alexandra's Birdwing · Chihuahua · Cat · Beaver · Rafflesia · Emperor Penguin · Chinese Giant Salamander

ANGEL FALLS

THE TALLEST WATERFALL ON EARTH

The average amount of water traveling over the falls every second could fill 30,000 plastic water bottles.

It is located in Venezuela. During warm weather, the water turns to mist before it hits the ground below.

It is about the same length as 120 blue whales lying nose to tail.

Uluru changes color depending on how the sun shines on it. Sometimes it looks brown or orange. At dawn and dusk, it glows bright red.

ULURU

A HUGE SANDSTONE ROCK IN AUSTRALIA

8-Year-Old Child · Giant Earthworm · Wandering Albatross · Elephant · Tyrannosaurus Rex · **Blue Whale** · **Redwood Tree** · **Angel Falls** · **Uluru** · Humongous Fungus · Mount Everest · Mariana Trench · Grand Canyon · Olympus Mons · Moon · Earth · Jupiter · Sun · VY Canis Majoris · The Solar System · Crab Nebula · Tarantula Nebula · Milky Way Galaxy · BOSS Great Wall

BIGGER

HUMONGOUS FUNGUS

A GIANT UNDERGROUND FUNGUS CHAIN THAT IS THE LARGEST LIVING THING ON EARTH

Humongous Fungus grows by eating the roots of trees.

Mushrooms are a common type of fungus, but beware! Only certain kinds of fungus are safe to eat.

No plants or animals live at the top because the air is so cold and hard to breathe.

MOUNT EVEREST

EARTH'S HIGHEST MOUNTAIN

SMALLER

Quark · Electron · Proton and Neutron · Atom · DNA Unit · Common Cold Virus · X Chromosome · White Blood Cell · Thickness of a Human Hair · Grain of Sand · Largest Bacteria · Snow Crystal · Ant · Poison Dart Frog · Chicken Egg · Apple · Hercules Beetle · Ear of Corn · Queen Alexandra's Birdwing · Chihuahua · Cat · Beaver · Rafflesia · Emperor Penguin · Chinese Giant Salamander

MARIANA TRENCH

THE DEEPEST PART OF THE OCEAN

If Mount Everest was dropped into the bottom of Mariana Trench, its tip would still be over one mile (1.6 kilometers) underwater.

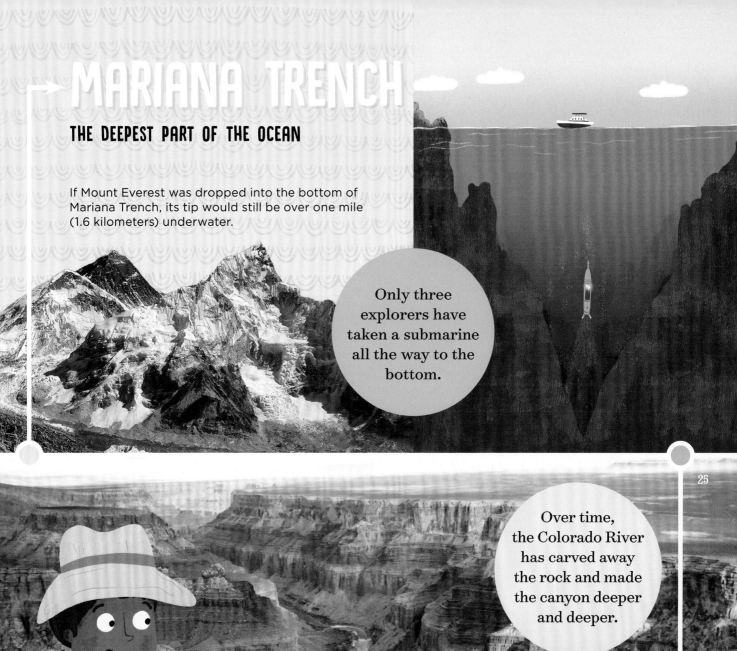

Only three explorers have taken a submarine all the way to the bottom.

Over time, the Colorado River has carved away the rock and made the canyon deeper and deeper.

The Grand Canyon is so big that different parts of it can experience different weather at the same time.

GRAND CANYON

A LONG, DEEP VALLEY IN THE US STATE OF ARIZONA

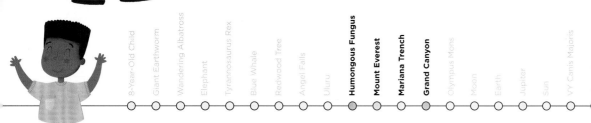

8-Year-Old Child • Giant Earthworm • Wandering Albatross • Elephant • Tyrannosaurus Rex • Blue Whale • Redwood Tree • Angel Falls • Uluru • **Humongous Fungus** • **Mount Everest** • **Mariana Trench** • **Grand Canyon** • Olympus Mons • Moon • Earth • Jupiter • Sun • VY Canis Majoris • The Solar System • Crab Nebula • Tarantula Nebula • Milky Way Galaxy • BOSS Great Wall • BIGGER

OLYMPUS MONS

THE TALLEST VOLCANO IN OUR SOLAR SYSTEM

Olympus Mons is located on Mars.

Olympus Mons is three times taller than Mount Everest.

The moon's gravity causes ocean waves to go in and out at the beach here on Earth.

Twelve people have walked on the moon.

MOON

A LARGE ROCK THAT CIRCLES THE EARTH AND REFLECTS THE SUN'S LIGHT, GIVING US LIGHT AT NIGHT

SMALLER

Quark
Electron
Proton and Neutron
Atom
DNA Unit
Common Cold Virus
X Chromosome
White Blood Cell
Thickness of a Human Hair
Grain of Sand
Largest Bacteria
Snow Crystal
Ant
Poison Dart Frog
Chicken Egg
Apple
Hercules Beetle
Ear of Corn
Queen Alexandra's Birdwing
Chihuahua
Cat
Beaver
Rafflesia
Emperor Penguin
Chinese Giant Salamander

EARTH

OUR HOME

Earth is the only planet we know of with oceans of water on its surface.

The Earth spins around once every 24 hours and takes 365 days to travel around the sun. That's where we get our days and years!

About 50 moons could fit inside the Earth.

The storm on Jupiter is larger than the size of two Earths.

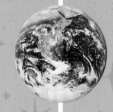

The huge red spot on Jupiter is a storm that has raged for hundreds of years.

JUPITER

THE LARGEST PLANET IN OUR SOLAR SYSTEM

8-Year-Old Child · Giant Earthworm · Wandering Albatross · Elephant · Tyrannosaurus Rex · Blue Whale · Redwood Tree · Angel Falls · Uluru · Humongous Fungus · Mount Everest · Mariana Trench · Grand Canyon · **Olympus Mons** · **Moon** · **Earth** · **Jupiter** · Sun · VY Canis Majoris · The Solar System · Crab Nebula · Tarantula Nebula · Milky Way Galaxy · BOSS Great Wall

BIGGER

SUN

THE STAR THAT GIVES US LIGHT AND HEAT AND HOLDS OUR SOLAR SYSTEM TOGETHER

One million Earths could fit inside the sun.

Light from the sun takes about eight minutes to reach Earth.

VY Canis Majoris is way bigger than our sun. In fact, 9.3 billion suns could fit inside it!

Canis Majoris means "the Great Dog."

If VY Canis Majoris were in our solar system, it would reach past the orbit of Jupiter.

VY CANIS MAJORIS

ONE OF THE LARGEST STARS

SMALLER

Quark · Electron · Proton and Neutron · Atom · DNA Unit · Common Cold Virus · X Chromosome · White Blood Cell · Thickness of a Human Hair · Grain of Sand · Largest Bacteria · Snow Crystal · Ant · Poison Dart Frog · Chicken Egg · Apple · Hercules Beetle · Ear of Corn · Queen Alexandra's Birdwing · Chihuahua · Cat · Beaver · Rafflesia · Emperor Penguin · Chinese Giant Salamander

THE SOLAR SYSTEM

THE EIGHT PLANETS THAT GO AROUND OUR SUN

The planets in our solar system are Mercury, Venus, Earth, Mars, Jupiter, Saturn, Uranus, and Neptune.

Voyager 1 was the first spacecraft to reach the edge of the solar system. It had to travel for almost 35 years.

It is expanding by about 1,500 kilometers every second. That's like growing by the size of one Earth every eight seconds!

In AD 1054, Chinese astronomers saw a star explode and create this nebula.

Nebulas are called star nurseries because new stars are born there.

CRAB NEBULA

A HUGE, COLORFUL CLOUD OF GAS AND DUST

8-Year-Old Child · Giant Earthworm · Wandering Albatross · Elephant · Tyrannosaurus Rex · Blue Whale · Redwood Tree · Angel Falls · Uluru · Humongous Fungus · Mount Everest · Mariana Trench · Grand Canyon · Olympus Mons · Moon · Earth · Jupiter · **Sun** · **VY Canis Majoris** · **The Solar System** · **Crab Nebula** · Tarantula Nebula · Milky Way Galaxy · BOSS Great Wall

BIGGER

TARANTULA NEBULA

THE LARGEST NEBULA

This nebula got its name because it looks like a giant spider. Good thing it's way out in space!

Galaxies form many different shapes. The Milky Way is a spiral galaxy. It looks like a pinwheel.

The Milky Way is made of 100 to 400 billion stars.

MILKY WAY GALAXY

THE GALAXY OUR SOLAR SYSTEM IS IN

SMALLER

Quark

Electron

Proton and Neutron

Atom

DNA Unit

Common Cold Virus

X Chromosome

White Blood Cell

Thickness of a Human Hair

Grain of Sand

Largest Bacteria

Snow Crystal

Ant

Poison Dart Frog

Chicken Egg

Apple

Hercules Beetle

Ear of Corn

Queen Alexandra's Birdwing

Chihuahua

Cat

Beaver

Rafflesia

Emperor Penguin

Chinese Giant Salamander

BOSS GREAT WALL

THE LARGEST STRUCTURE IN THE UNIVERSE THAT WE KNOW ABOUT

The largest thing in the universe is actually super far away from us. The universe is that big!

And there are probably even bigger things out there that we don't know about and might never know about but that were created just to make God happy.

Doesn't it blow your mind that God is even bigger than the entire universe? He has to be bigger because he's the one who designed and created it all. And even though he is so big, he still sees and knows and loves YOU!

This galaxy supercluster may seem like the boss of the universe, but its name doesn't come from its size. It stands for **B**aryon **O**scillation **S**pectroscopic **S**urvey, which is much harder to say than BOSS.

Scientists have counted 830 galaxies in the BOSS Great Wall, but there are probably many more.

The BOSS Great Wall is a HUMONGOUS group of galaxies in space, and our Milky Way galaxy isn't even in it. Isn't that amazing?

31

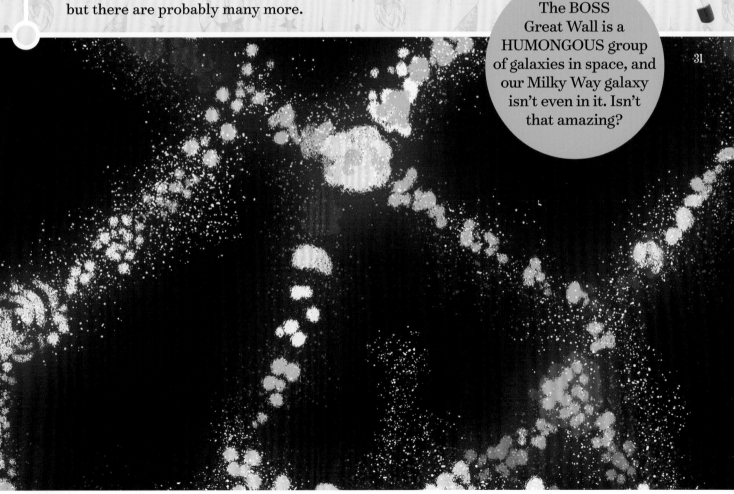

8-Year-Old Child · Giant Earthworm · Wandering Albatross · Elephant · Tyrannosaurus Rex · Blue Whale · Redwood Tree · Angel Falls · Uluru · Humongous Fungus · Mount Everest · Mariana Trench · Grand Canyon · Olympus Mons · Moon · Earth · Jupiter · Sun · VY Canis Majoris · The Solar System · Crab Nebula · **Tarantula Nebula** · **Milky Way Galaxy** · **BOSS Great Wall**

BIGGER

INDEX OF SIZES

Quarks and electrons are so small that scientists call them point particles, which means they have zero size when they are measured.

Diameter of a Proton and Neutron: 1×10^{-15} meters

Diameter of an Atom: $\sim 1 \times 10^{-10}$ meters

Length of a DNA Unit: $\sim 6 \times 10^{-10}$ meters

Length of a Common Cold Virus: $\sim 3 \times 10^{-8}$ meters

Length of an X Chromosome: 7×10^{-6} meters

Diameter of a White Blood Cell: 1.2×10^{-5} meters

Thickness of a Human Hair: $\sim 1 \times 10^{-4}$ meters

Diameter of a Grain of Sand: $\sim 5 \times 10^{-4}$ meters

Length of the Largest Bacteria: ~0.75 millimeters

Diameter of a Snow Crystal: ~1 millimeter

Length of an Ant: ~4 millimeters

Length of a Poison Dart Frog: ~3.8 centimeters

Length of a Chicken Egg: ~5.5 centimeters

Diameter of an Apple: ~8.5 centimeters

Length of a Hercules Beetle: ~17.3 centimeters

Length of an Ear of Corn: ~19 centimeters

Wingspan of a Queen Alexandra's Birdwing: ~27 centimeters

Length of a Chihuahua: ~30 centimeters

Length of a Cat: ~45 centimeters

Length of a Beaver: ~80 centimeters

Diameter of a Rafflesia: ~91 centimeters

Height of an Emperor Penguin: ~1.1 meters

Length of a Chinese Giant Salamander: ~1.2 meters

Height of an Eight-Year-Old Child: ~1.25 meters

Length of a Giant Earthworm: ~2 meters

Wingspan of a Wandering Albatross: ~3.4 meters

Length of an Elephant: ~4 meters

Length of a Tyrannosaurus Rex: ~12 meters

Length of a Blue Whale: ~30 meters

Height of a Redwood Tree: ~107 meters

Height of Angel Falls: 979 meters

Length of Uluru: 3.6 kilometers

Length of Humongous Fungus: ~3.8 kilometers

Height of Mount Everest: 8.8 kilometers

Depth of Mariana Trench: 11 kilometers

Length of Grand Canyon: 446 kilometers

Diameter of Olympus Mons: 624 kilometers

Diameter of the Moon: 3,474 kilometers

Diameter of the Earth: 12,742 kilometers

Diameter of Jupiter: 139,820 kilometers

Diameter of the Sun: 1.39 million kilometers

Diameter of VY Canis Majoris: 1.98 billion kilometers

Diameter of the Solar System: ~287.5 billion kilometers

Diameter of the Crab Nebula: ~104.1 trillion kilometers

Diameter of the Tarantula Nebula: $\sim 1.76 \times 10^{16}$ kilometers

Diameter of the Milky Way Galaxy: ~105,700 light-years

Diameter of the BOSS Great Wall: ~1 billion light-years

DEFINITIONS

Depth:	measuring something from its top surface to its bottom
Diameter:	drawing a line through the middle of something and measuring that line from one end to the other
Height:	measuring something from its bottom to its top
Length:	measuring something from one end to the other
Wingspan:	measuring an animal from the tip of one wing to the tip of the other